PRACTICAL HANDBOOK OF SOCIAL PHARMACY ER-20

Strictly as per new PCI norms recognized as ER-20-15P (R.G.P.V) Syllabus for diploma in pharmacy first-year students

Mr. Akhilesh Gupta
B. Pharm, M. Pharm, Ph.D*
Assistant Professor,
BM College of Pharmaceutical
Education and Research, Indore, Madhya Pradesh, India

Mr. Chintaman Kumawat
B. Pharm, M. Pharm,
Associate Professor,
Shri Bherulal Pharmacy Institute,
Madhya Pradesh, India

Mr. Umesh K. Atneriya
B. Pharm, M. Pharm, Ph.D*
Associate Professor,
BM College of Pharmaceutical
Education and Research, Indore, Madhya Pradesh, India

NOTION PRESS

Copyright © Feb 2023 Umesh K. Atneriya

All rights reserved

DEDICATION

This book is dedicated to our parents, Colleagues, friends and almighty god.

Preface

The practical handbook of Social Pharmacy has been written for students of diploma in pharmacy first-year students keeping in mind specific requirements of the Pharmacy Council of India (PCI), Education Regulation - 2020. This practical book is covering the entire practical syllabus of social pharmacy as per new PCI norms recognized as ER-20-15P. This practical handbook containing fourteen experiments. In preceding practical book describe the roles and responsibilities of pharmacists in various National health programs, various health hazards including microbial sources, advice on preventive measures for various diseases, provide first aid for various emergency conditions including basic life support and cardiopulmonary resuscitation and design promotional materials for public health awareness have discussed. This practical book is basically health education and community pharmacy. I would like to acknowledge the invaluable contributions provided by the Notion press editorial team. I give great thanks to the graphic designers who were instrumental in preparing much of the artwork for this text. I would also like to acknowledge my colleagues and students for their willingness to serve as test subjects for many of the useful contents in this practical book. Finally, I would like to thank my teachers and parents for their guidance, support, and encouragement throughout the process of completing this practical book.

The Practical handbook will certainly contribute to the enhancement of the skills and competency with the professional services at the level of national health.

Mr. Akhilesh Gupta, M.Pharm
Mr. Chintaman Kumawat, M.Pharm
Mr. Umesh K. Atneriya, M. Pharm.

List of Contents

EXPERIMENT NO. {01}

Object: To study national immunization schedule for children, adult vaccine schedule, vaccines which are not included in the national immunization program.

References:

1) Murgesh N. Health Education and Community Pharmacy, Sataya sai publisher fourth edition reprint in 2006.

2) Parmar N. S. Health Education and Community Pharmacy CBS Publisher and distributors reprint in 2007.

Theory :-

Vaccination is a proven and one of the most cost-effective child survival interventions. All countries in the world have an immunization programme to deliver selected vaccines to the targeted beneficiaries, specially focusing on pregnant women, infants and children, who are at a high risk of diseases preventable by vaccines. Vaccine is the chemical substances or biological preparation which provides the active acquired immunity against any disease. Generally vaccine contains the resemble microorganism or chemical substances (toxins, surface protein etc.) in inactive/killed form. During the vaccination, vaccine are injected in the body, after that it behaves as a antigen or foreign substance to the body, so our body work against this substances and produced the antibodies create a immunity. It is called that primary response against disease. After that immunity are developed and stored in the memory cells of the brain regarding to the previous infections. In future any similar infections are cause then our immune system give rapid response and fight against disease this is called secondary response by producing antibodies. Vaccines play a major role in prophylactic and therapeutic role in many diseases.

Antigen— Antigens are those substances that stimulate the immune system to produce antibodies (protective body). It behaves like foreign particles (bacteria, virus) for recipient body and cause undesirable changes, then recipient body protects itself by producing the antibodies.

Antibody—Antibody is the proteinaceous protective modification produced by the immune system in response to the presence of the foreign substances like bacteria, viruses etc and neutralize their activities.

Types of vaccine:

- Live attenuated vaccine (LAV)
- Inactivated vaccine (Killed vaccine)

- Subunit vaccine (Purified antigen)
- Toxoid vaccine (Inactivated Toxoid)

Vaccine research and development:

The research and development of vaccines for locally prevalent diseases like pneumonia, diarrhea, JE, dengue, cholera, typhoid and diseases like leishmaniasis etc. in India should be given a priority.

India has a number of institutions, where vaccine related projects are executed i.e.

- Indian Council of Medical Research (ICMR)
- Department of Science and Technology (DST)
- Council for Scientific and Industrial Research (CSIR)

Objectives of the national vaccine policy:

- To contribute to prevention of mortality and morbidity due to communicable diseases.
- To ensure consistent delivery and administration of vaccines to everyone in need.
- To synergize all relevant policies for effective implementation of the national vaccine policy.
- To achieve national self-reliance in vaccine R&D.
- To develop and use the interdisciplinary knowledge base.
- To achieve pre-eminence in the capabilities of the indigenous public sector for self-reliance.
- To develop a system for monitoring and compensating AEFI.
- To promote ethical conduct in the development, trials, adoption and administration of vaccines.
- To enable India to play a leading role in the supply of affordable vaccines.

Immunization Programme

In May 1974, WHO started the Expanded Programme on Immunization (EPI) to bring six antigens to all the children of the world through improved management training of health personnel and development of effective cold chain to maintain vaccine potency.EPI was adopted by Government of India in 1978 to reduce the incidence of common infectious disease in childhood which are tuberculosis, diphtheria, tetanus, pertusis, polio and measles.

In 1985, the Universal Immunization Programme (UPI) was lanched, which aims at immunizing all children before their first birthday against the six vaccine preventable disease. Under UPI the emphasis is on the "under five". Universal immunization was hoped to be achieved by 1990. UPI is aimed at adding impetus to the global programme of EPI.

UIP was given the status of a national technology mission in 1986. A specific immunization strengthening project was designed to run from 2000-2003,whichincluded three main components

- ➢ Polio eradication
- ➢ Strengthening routine immunization
- ➢ Strategic framework for development

Cold Chain System

Vaccines are sensitive to heat. On exposure to heat their potency is lost. Once a vaccine has lost its potency it cannot be regained, so it is important to maintain cold chain

National Immunization Schedule

Immunization Schedule

Age	Vaccine	Hepatitis B	
At birth or soon thereafter	BCG, OPV		
6 weeks	DPT, OPV		
10 weeks	DPT, OPV		
14 weeks	DPT, OPV	5 years	DT
9 months	OPV, Measles	10 years	DT
18-24 months	DPT (Booster)	16 years	TT
	OPT (Booster)		

- ➢ If born in hospital, BCG vaccination may be administered at birth or before discharge.
- ➢ If delivery takes place in an institution, given an additional dose of OPV before baby is discharged. But do not count this dose, it is known was dose of OPV.

Vaccines in the Adult Immunization Schedule

- ✓ Hepatitis A
- ✓ Hepatitis B
- ✓ Haemophilusinfluenzae type b
- ✓ Human papillomavirus
- ✓ Influenza

- ✓ Measles, mumps, rubella
- ✓ Meningococcal ACWY
- ✓ Meningococcal B
- ✓ Pneumococcal
- ✓ Tetanus, diphtheria, whooping cough
- ✓ Varicella
- ✓ Zoster

Nursing Responsibils While Administering Immunization

- Use one sterile syringe and needle for each injection.
- Use only the diluents with measles and BCG vaccine.
- Start immunization with polio vaccine, and then administer other vaccines.
- Observe strict aseptic precaution while administer other vaccines.
- Educate parents/guardians regarding the following aspects:

Barriers to strengthen immunization programme

- Lack of a financial sustainability plan for the introduction of new vaccines.
- Limited economic evaluations.
- Lack of baseline surveillance data.
- Lack of diagnostic tools and specialized training for certain VPD.
- Lack of data on disease burden in India.

Adverse events following immunization surveillance system

The Central Drug Laboratory used for testing for vaccine samples in AEFI are

- ➢ Central Drugs Testing Laboratory, Mumbai, Maharashtra, India
- ➢ Central Drugs Laboratory, Kolkata, West Bengal, India
- ➢ Central Drugs Testing Laboratory, Chennai, Tamil Nadu, India
- ➢ Central Drugs Testing Laboratory, Hyderabad, Andhra Pradesh, India
- ➢ Central Drugs Laboratory, Central Research Institute, Kasauli, H.P., India
- ➢ Regional Drugs Testing Laboratory, Guwahati, Assam, India
- ➢ Regional Drugs Testing Laboratory, Chandigarh, India

Result:

EXPERIMENT NO. {02}

Object:-To study of RCH – reproductive and child health- nutritional aspects.

References:

1) Murgesh N. Health Education and Community Pharmacy, Sataya sai publisher fourth edition reprint in 2006.

2) Parmar N. S. Health Education and Community Pharmacy CBS Publisher and distributors reprint in 2007.

Theory:-

In order to grow and stay healthy, young children need a variety of nutritious food such as Fruits, Fresh vegetables, Brest milk ,Meat, Fish, Pulses, Grains, Eggs, as well as grains. A child stomach is smaller than an adult's, so child cannot eat as much at one meal. But children's energy and body building needs are great.

There are 5 aspect of nutrition: - 05 Essential Nutrients to maximize your health.

1) **Carbohydrate:-** carbohydrate are either simple or complex and are major sources of energy in all human diets . They are composed of Carbon, Hydrogen and Oxygen.

    Examples:- Glucose, fructose (in fruits), vegetables, glycogen in animal foods.

2) **Proteins:-** Proteins are primary structural and functional components of every living cells. Proteins are composed of Carbon, Nitrogen, Oxygen, Hydrogen and Sulpher.

    Examples:- Milk , Egg, meat, fish, pulses, legumes etc are rich sources of proteins .

3) **Fats:-** Fats are concentrated sources of energy made up of fatty acids in different proportions.

    Examples :- Oils, butter, ghee and other dietary products.

4) **Vitamins and Minerals:-** vitamins are chemical compounds required by the body in a small amounts. **Examples of Vitamins:-** Vit. A, Vit B, Vit. C etc.

    Mineral are inorganic elements found in body fluids and tissues.

    Examples of Minerals:- sodium ,potassium, calcium, phosphorus, copper, zinc

5) **Water:-** Water, a substances composed of the chemical elements hydrogen and oxygen and existing in gaseous, liquid and solid states. Formula: - H_2O

6) **Reproductive Health**:- Reproductive health is a state of complete physical, mental and social well-being and not merely the absence of disease or infirmity, in all matters relating to the reproductive system and to its functions and processes.

There are some important vitamins, which is essential for healthy life:-

<u>TABLE :-</u> **chart on nutrients , sources of various nutrients from locally available foods .**

Fat soluble vitamins :-

S.NO	Vitamins and its chemical names	Sources	Deficiency Diseases	Daily Requirments
01	Vit. A retinol	Milk, egg, green leafy vegetables.	Stunted growth ,night blindness,xerophthalmia, keratinization	750 mcg
02	Vit. D calciferol	Fish liver oils, milk, egg yolk	Rickets ,osteomalacia	2.5 mcg
03	Vit. E tocopherols	Egg yolk, green vegetabls, nuts,butter	Cystic fibrosis, ataxia,crohn's disease	8-10 mg
04	Vit. K phylloquinone	Cabbage, fruits,leafy vegetables,	Slow blood clotting ,hemorrhages in new born	70-140 g

<u>TABLE</u> **:- chart on nutrients , sources of various nutrients from locally available foods**

water soluble vitamins :-

S.NO.	Vitamins and its chemical names	Sources	Deficiency Diseases	Daily Requirments
01	Vit. B_1 thiamin	Nuts, legumes yeast, egg yolk	Beri-beri	1-1.5 mg
02	Vit.B_2 r Riboflavin	Milk, green vegetables,eggs, liver	Dermatitis ,angular stomatitis	1.5-2 mg
03	Vit. B_6Pyridoxine	egg yolk ,liver, beans,soyabeans meat	Rarely observed	1-2 mg
04	Folic acid	green vegetables,eggs, liver	Anemia	200 g
05	Nicotinic acid or niacin	Yeast, fish,pulses	Pellegra, Dermatitis, dementia	10-20 mg
06	Pantothenic acid	egg yolk ,liver, green vegetables, liver	Dermatitis, adrenal insufficiency	Unknown
07	Biotin	Yeast, liver, pulses,nuts	Dermatitis,conjunct ivitis	Unknown
08	Vit. C or Ascorbic acid	Citrus fruits, berries,lemon.	Hemorrhages, scurvy,anaemia,slo w wound healing.	30-45 mg

Results :-

Object: To study Family planning devices.

References :-

1) Gupta k. Ashok, "Health Education and community pharmacy", Published by CBS publishers and distributors Pvt. Ltd., Edition~1st 1996.

2) Murgesh N. Health Education and Community Pharmacy, Sataya sai publisher fourth edition reprint in 2006.

Theory:

Pharmacists being members of health team are well aware of the danger of population explosion and hence they can realize the need of population control and the importance of family planning.

Family planning refers to practices that help individual or couples to attain the following **objectives:**

> ➢ To avoid unwanted births and bring about wanted births.
> ➢ To regulate the spacing between children.
> ➢ To control the time at which births occur in relation to the age of parents.

According to WHO, family planning is a way of thinking and living that is adopted voluntary, upon the basic of knowledge, attitudes and responsive decisions by individuals and couples, in order to promote the health and welfare of the family group and thus contributes effectively to the social development of a country.

Scope

Family planning has a wide scope and includes the following activities:

> ➢ Proper spacing and limitation of birth.
> ➢ Investigations and advice on sterility.
> ➢ Education for parenthood.
> ➢ Sex education.
> ➢ Screening of the reproductive system for pathological conditions.
> ➢ Genetic counseling.
> ➢ Premarital consultations and examinations.
> ➢ Carrying out pregnancy tests.

Contraception Methods

Contraception methods are used to avoid unwanted pregnancies resulting from citrus. They are also used as fertility regulating methods. An ideal contraceptive should be safe, effective, and acceptable to both of the partners, reversible, cheap, easily available and easy to use, indecent of coitus, long lasting, free from side effects and should not require medical supervision. Each of the contraceptive methods or devices had its own advantages and disadvantages and adoption of particular methods in purely a matter of individual couple's preference.

Contraceptive methods can be classified as follows –

Behavioral methods

These are simplest and their success depends on how the two parterres to coitus behave.

- **Abstinence**

This is the most effective contraceptive method but not practical. It means that one should abstain from sex act which is probably unnatural and may lead to temperamental changes and even nervous breakdown.

- **Coitus interrupts**

This method is based on interruption during coitus. During the coitus the male partner withdraws his panis from female passage just before ejaculation and discharge outside. The deposition of the semen into the vegina is prevented. Thus coitus interrupts is an voluntary method and does not involve cost or appliance. However some couples find it difficult in practice.

- **Rhythm method**

It is also called as 'safe period' or 'calendar method' first described in 1930. Coitus is performed 7 to 8 days before and after menstrual flow. The method is based on the fact that ovulation occurs from 12 to 16 days before the onset menstruation.

Physical method

- **Condom**

Condom and sheaths meet the requirement of an ideal contraception. Condom is most popular in india. Most outstanding advantage of condom is that it protects both the partners from sexually transmitted diseases. It is made from latex. The condom is applied on the erect penis before intercourse, air removed from the teat and withdrawn from the vegina carefully after intercourse to avoid spilling of semen in the vagina.

- **Diaphragm**

Diaphragms and cervical caps are available in various designs for use of females but require prior training. The combined used of diaphragm has to be with spermicidal jelly enhances the safety from contraception. The diaphragm has to be inserted before sexual intercourse and must remain in place for at least 6 hours after intercourse.

- **Vaginal sponge**

It is small polyurethane foam sponge saturated with a spermicidal. It is very less effective than diaphragm and not used in India.

Chemical methods

In conventional methods a spermicide is incorporated in the base and the product is used as

- Foam tablets or foam aerosols.
- Cream, jellies.
- Suppositories.
- Soluble films.

Result

EXPERIMENT NO. {04}

Objec:- To study of different microscopically observation of different microbes.

References:-

1) Gupta k. Ashok, "Health Education and community pharmacy", Published by CBS publishers and distributors Pvt. Ltd., Edition~1st 1996.

2) Murgesh N. Health Education and Community Pharmacy, Sataya sai publisher fourth edition reprint in 2006.

Theory:- Microbes are single cell organisms that are invisible to necked eye. Microbes are unicellular organisms. The tem microbes used to describes several different live forms with different size and characteristics. They make up of almost 60% of deaths living.

Some examples of microbes are :-

(1) Bacteria

(2) Viruses

(3) Fungi

(4) Archea

(5) Protozoa

(1) Bacteria

Bacteria are unicellular microscopic prokaryotic microbes organisms that contain nucleus, they are made-up of peptidoglycane cell wall, DNA and having flagella.

(A) Based on gram staining

Bacteria are differentiated into 2 groups :-

    (1) Gram positive bacteria :-   Staphylococcus, Streptococcus, Clostridium

    (2) Gram negetive bacteria :-   Escherichia, Salmonela, Vibrio, Protius

(B)   Based on shape of bacteria:- cocci, bacilli, vibrios, actinomycities, vibriosetc.

    Viruses:- viruses are connecting link between living and nonliving organisms,they contain either DNA or RNA ,they are non-cellular composed of protein, nucleic acid and lipids. Example:- HIV , NOVEL CORONA VIRUS etc.

    Fungi:- Fungi cause a variety of diseases. They are eukaryotic protiest which differ from in several protists which differ from bacteria in several ways. Fungi are eukaryotic microorganisms. Fungi can occuras yeasts, molds, as a combination of both forms.

Diseases :- Fungal nail infection, Vaginal candidiasis, Ringworm, Candida infections of the mouth, throat and esophagus, jock itch, yeast infection, skin fungal infections.

 For example :- Aspergillus, Clavaria, Neurospora Crassa, Peziza, Cyathus, Xylaria.

(3) **Archea:-** They are unicellular prokaryotic organisms and have structure similar to bacteria. Their cell wall is different from bacteria and contains unit of lipids .These microoganisms lack cell nuclei and are therefore prokaryotes .

(4) **Protozoa:-** Protozoa are single celled or unicellular organisms, which are microscopic in size, Which include amoebas, flagellates,ciliates,sporozones, and many other forms.

Diseases :- Amoebiasis, Babesiosis,Giardiasis,Lambliasis,Malaria etc.

Example:- Balantidium coli, Trypanosoma Gambiense, Giardia Intestinalis etc.

Results :-

EXPERIMENT NO. {5}

Object: To study oral health and hygiene.

References :-

1) Gupta k. Ashok, "Health Education and community pharmacy", Published by CBS publishers and distributors Pvt. Ltd., Edition~1st 1996.

2) Murgesh N. Health Education and Community Pharmacy, Sataya sai publisher fourth edition reprint in 2006.

Theory:

The oral cavity is known to be a reservoir for pathogens to grow and thrive. Poor oral hygiene can lead to complications such as gingivitis, halitosis, xerostomia, plaque formation and dental caries. Chest infection and pneumonia with poor oral hygiene. The various diseases/conditions like diabetes, renal failure, malnutrition and dehydration and being on oxygen therapy, cancer therapy, immunosuppressive drugs, and antibiotic or phenytoin treatment increases an individual's risk of oral complications. Therefore, such patients will require more attention to their oral hygiene. Care of the mouth is an important nursing procedure and should be performed as part of the routine general hygiene of a patient. Nurses play an important role in providing effective oral care and promoting oral hygiene.

Various Types Of Complications Occurs Due To Poor Oral Hygiene

- **Oral hygiene:**The condition or practice of maintaining the tissues and structures of the mouth in healthy state.

- **Dental caries:**

A plaque-induced disease caused by the complex interaction of food, especially starches and sugars, with bacteria that form dental plaque.

- **Debris:**

The dead, diseased or damaged tissue and any foreign material that is to be removed from a wound or other area being treated.

- **Gingivitis:**

A condition in which the gingival margin around the teeth may be red, swollen, and bleeding.

- **Dental plaque:**

A biofilm composed of microorganisms that attaches with acquired pellicle (crust) to the teeth and causes dental caries and infections of the gingival tissue.

Halitosis:

Offensive breath commonly caused by poor oral hygiene, dental or oral infections.

- **Xerostomia:**

Dryness of the mouth caused by reduced saliva secretion.

Methods for Maintaining Oral Hygiene

1. Tooth brushes

2. Foam Swabs

3. Mouth Square

Toothbrushes

Tooth brushing should be the first line of oral cleansing method unless the patient is prone to bleeding, pain or aspiration.

Rationale:

1. Tooth brushing removes more plaque and cleans a proximal and crevice sites better than foam swabs.

2. Tooth brushing is an effective means of reducing plaque and gingivitis.

3. It is most economical.

Frequency of Tooth brushing

Brush teeth at least twice a day, preferably soon after awakening in the morning and before going to bed.

Rationale:

1. Use soft-bristled, small-ended toothbrush.

❖ **Foam Swabs**

Use foam swabs/brushes with chlorhexidine or toothpaste when tooth brushing is not advisable. For example, in the elderly or patients with bleeding tendency.

Rationale:

1. Use of toothbrush in a geriatric person can cause irritation and trauma to sensitive tissues more readily and reduce the effectiveness of oral care.

2. Foam swabs are less abrasive and reduces further trauma to the oral cavity.

❖ **Mouth Square**

Do not use mouth square/cotton square/gauze.

Rationale:

Cleansing with gauze, even when performed four hourly, exerts only transient effects, and is ineffective in removing debris.

Oral Cleansing Agents

- Fluoride Toothpaste
- Glycerine-Based Products
- Glycerine-Based Products With Lemon
- Sodium Bicarbonate
- Hydrogen Peroxide
- Chlorhexidine Mouthwash
- Normal Saline Mouthwash

Result:

EXPERIMENT NO. {06}

Object:-To study of personal hygiene and etiquettes. [Hand washing, various types of masks, PPE gear.

References:-

1) Gupta k. Ashok, "Health Education and community pharmacy", Published by CBS publishers and distributors Pvt. Ltd., Edition 1st 1996.

2) Murgesh N. Health Education and Community Pharmacy, Sataya sai publisher fourth edition reprint in 2006.

Theory:-hygiene is typically thought of in terms of proper hand washing, body washing, and facial cleanliness. Although these practices are interrupting the spread of disease, another component of good hygiene consists of practicing good hygiene etiquette.

Personal hygiene includes:-

A . Cleaning your body every day

B. Washing your hands with soap or sanitizer.

C. Brushing your teeth twice a day.

D. Covering your mouth and nose by mask when sneezing and coughing.

E. Washing your hands after handling pets and other animals.

Importance of Hygiene:-

1) Good hygiene habits help us to keep our body strong and healthy.

2) Cleanliness helps to prevent diseases.

3) It also helps us to good appearance.

4) Good hygiene hobbits helps us to keep our body free from germs and disease free.

5) It helped us have better self esteem.

Hand Washing Technique

Follow these five steps every time:-

1. WET:- wet your hands with clean, running water, turn off the tap and apply soap.

2. LATHER:- lather youe hands by rubbing them together with the soap . lather the backs of your hands, between your fingers and under your nails .

3. SCRUB :- srub your hands for at least 20 seconds.

4. RINSE:- rinse your hands well under clean, running water .

5. DRY:- dry your hands using a clean towel or air dry them.

Various Types of Masks:-

1) **Disposable surgical mask** :- these flat, thin, paper-like masks are usually white and light blue. Surgical face masks can filter out about 60% of smaller, inhaled particles.

2) **N95, KN95 MASK :-** KN95 respirators are made to china specification and standards and N95 are made to U.S. design standards. Both are rated to filter out 95% of very small particles. Both respirators protected against novel corona virus and other respiratory diseases.

2) **HOMEMADE CLOTH MASK: -** A two layer cotton mask filter out about 35% of small particles.

PPE GEAR:-

Personal protective Equipment (PPE) is used to reduce the risk of droplets transmission of infection to the wearer. PPE refers to protective clothing, helmets, gloves, face shields, goggles, facemasks and or respirators to protect the wearer from infections or viral diseases.

USES :-

1) PPE is used to reduce the risk of droplets transmission of infection to the wearer.

2) PPE is used to reduce the risk of droplets transmission of infection to others.

Results :-

EXPERIMENT NO. {07}

Object:-To study of different menstrual products.

References:-

1) Gupta k. Ashok, "Health Education and community pharmacy", Published by CBS publishers and distributors Pvt. Ltd., Edition~1st 1996.

2) Murgesh N. Health Education and Community Pharmacy, Sataya sai publisher fourth edition reprint in 2006.

Theory:- Those products that are used during menstruation may also be called menstrual hygiene products. Feminine hygiene products also include products meant to cleanse the vulva or vagina such as douches, feminine wipes soap. Feminine hygiene products that are meant to cleanse may lead to allergic reaction and irritation, as the vagina naturally flushes out bacteria. Feminine hygiene products are either disposable or reusable.

1) Disposable products:- sanitary napkins, tampons and pantyliners are disposable.

2) Reusable products:- menstrual cups, cloth menstrual pads, period panties are reusable.

1) Disposable products :-

A) Panty liner:- Stick to the inside of underwear to absorb blood and uterine lining during menstruation. **For example:-** sofy ,whisper etc.

B) **Sanitary napkins (pad):-** worn on the inside of underwear to absorb a heavier menstrual flow .Available in many different absorbencies and lengths with or without wings.

For example:- Stayfree, whisper,

C) Tampon:- Inserted inside the vagina to absorb menstrual blood, can also be used while swimming . Available in different level of absorbencies.

2) Reusable products:-

A) Menstrual cup:- Inserted inside the vagina to catch blood / uterine lining.

B) Cloth menstrual pad:- worn inside underwear.

C) Period panties:- can refer to either underwear that keeps pads in place or absorbent underwear that can take place of tampons and pads .

 3) Cleansing products:-

A) Douches:- A fluid used to flush out the inside of the vagina.

Feminine wipes:- A moist sometimes scented cloth used to wipe the vulva.

Results:-

EXPERIMENT NO. {08}

Object:-To study of marketed preparations of disinfectants, antiseptics, fumigating agents, antiviral agents, mosquito repellents etc.

References:-

1) Murgesh N. Health Education and Community Pharmacy, Sataya sai publisher fourth edition reprint in 2006.

3) Parmar N. S. Health Education and Community Pharmacy CBS Publisher and distributors reprint in 2007.

Theory:-:

Marketed Preparation: - The manner in which drug substances is presented in the market. (e.g. - solids, liquids or semi solids).

Disinfectants:- Disinfectants are chemical agents that are applied to non-living items to kill bacteria, viruses, fungi, mold, and mildews that are present.

For example:- Lysol, Harpic.

Antiseptics:- An antiseptic is an antimicrobial substance or compound that is applied to living tissue/ skin to reduce the possibility of infection, sepsis or putrefaction.

For examples:- Povidone iodine, Isopropyl alcohol, Hydrogen peroxide, Dettol etc.

Fumigating Agents :- fumigants, any volatile, poisonous substance used to kill insects, nematodes, and other animals or plants that damage stored foods or seeds, clothing and nursery stock.

For example :- Methyl bromide, Hydrogen cyanide, hydrogen phosphide, Ethylene dibromide etc.

Antiviral Agents:- Antiviral drugs are a class of medication used for treating viral infections. An agent that killa a virus or that suppresses its ability to replicate and hence, inhibits its capability to multiply and reproduce.

Antiviral diseases:- HIV, Ebola, Corona virus like covid 19, Swine flu.

Mosquito Repellents:- A mosquito repellent is a substance put on skin, clothing or other surface which discourages mosquitoes from landing or crawling on that surface.

For example :- Neem oil, All -out, Good-night , kachhua chhap agarbatti etc.

Results:-

Object:- To study of health communication : awareness on 5 different communicable diseases, their signs and symptoms and prevention.

References:-

1) Murgesh N. Health Education and Community Pharmacy, Sataya sai publisher fourth edition reprint in 2006.

2) Parmar N. S. Health Education and Community Pharmacy CBS Publisher and distributors reprint in 2007.

Theory:- A communicable disease is one that is spread from one person to another through a variety of ways that include: contact with blood and bodily fluids; breathing in an airborne virus; or by being bitten by an insect.

Five Communicable Diseases Their Signsand Symptoms:-

1)   **Common cold**: - rhinoviruses is responsible for common cold.

Signs and symptoms: - A stuffy or runny Sore throat, Headache, Fever, red and watery eyes.

Influenza:- Influenza viruses are infections that attack the respiratory system.

Signs and symptoms:-   Muscles or body aches, cough, A stuffy or runny , Sore throat, Headache, Fever, **fatigue.**

HIV:- HIV attacks the immune system of its host.A person can contact with blood or other body fluids containing the viruses.

Signs and symptoms:-   fever, Chills, Rash, Mouth sores, Sore throat, Swollen lymph nodes, Night sweats, Muscles aches, Fatigue.

2) **MMR :-** Measles, mumps, rubella is a contagious diseases that can lead to serious illness.

Signs and symptoms :-   A high fever , stuffy or runny nose, tiredness, a barky cough, red rash.

3) **Hepatitis A :-** A highly contagious liver infection caused by the hepatitis A virus.

Signs and symptoms :-fatigue, nausea, abdominal pain, loss of appetite and low grade fever, itching, diarrhea, vomiting, dark urine, jaundice.

<u>Results :-</u>

Object :- To study of water purification techniques, use of water testing kit, calculation of content/ percentage of $KMnO_4$, bleaching powder to be used for wells/ tanks and communication, counseling etc.

References:-

1) Gupta k. Ashok, "Health Education and community pharmacy", Published by CBS publishers and distributors Pvt. Ltd., Edition~1st 1996.

2) Murgesh N. Health Education and Community Pharmacy, Sataya sai publisher fourth edition reprint in 2006.

Theory:-   water purification is the process of removing undesirable chemicals, biological contaminants, suspended solids and gases from water. The goal is to produce water that is fit specific purposes. Most water is purified and disinfected for human consumption (drinking water), but water purification may also be carried out for a variety of other purposes, including medical, pharmacological, chemical and industrial applications.

There some water purification techniques:-

1) **Boiling: - The** simplest method to purify water is to boil it for a good time. High temperatures cause the bacteria and virus to dissipate, removing all impurities from the water. However, the dead micro-organisms and impurities settle at the bottom of the water. You must strain the water through a microporous sieve t completely remove the impurities.

2) **Water Purifier:-** An electric water purifier is the most trusted form of water purification found in most houses today. A water purifier uses a multi- stage process involving UV and UF filtration, carbon block and modern water filtration technology that eliminates most of the chemicals and impurities making it the purest drinking water.

3) **Reverse Osmosis (RO):-** An RO purifier proves to be one of the bestmethods of purifying water . RO forces water through a semipermeable membrane removes contaminates.

4) **Water Coronation:-** It is an order technique used usually during an emergency, wherein a mild bleach with approximately 5% chlorine is added to the water . This mixture works as an oxidant and quickly kills microorganisms, making water safe for consumption.

Distillation:- Distillation is water purification techniques involving collecting the condensed water after evaporation, ensuring that isnot as effective as an RO filter because it s the timeconsuming and eliminates minerals.

Use of Water Testing Kit:- Dirking water test kits indicate the presence of bacteria, pesticides and lead . Kits all include readings for nitrate (0 to 50 ppm), pH (6to 10), and water hardness (0 to 425 ppm).

Test:- Fill a test container with a water sample ,dip a test strip in , swirl the container ,and wait a few minutes with the test strip resting in the water sample. Take the strip out of the water and compare the color change on the test stripe to a color chart included in the kit.

calculatin of content/ percentage of $KMnO_4$: potassium permanganate, or $KMNO_4$, has a molar maas of 158 g/mol. (39+55+16*4)

$$\text{% Composition of K} : 39/158 = 0.247 = 24.7\%$$

$$\text{% Composition of Mn} : 55/158 = 34.8\%$$

$$\text{% Composition of O} : 64/158 = 0.405 = 40.5\%$$

Bleaching Powder to Be Used For Wells/Tanks :-

It is used to clean undreground sumps and overhead tanks. Take a bucket and add 400 geams of unitedlys bleaching powder in 10 lit. of water. Leave it for 02 min. Now, leaveing the residue, add only the solution into the tank and wash it completely.

Uses:-

    1) it is used in bleaching cotton.

    2) It is used as an oxidising agent in chemical industris.

    4)   It can be used for disinfecting water.

Communication And Counseling:- Direct purposes include bathing, drinking and cooking while examples of indirect purposes are the uses of water in processing wood to make paper and in producing steel for automobiles. The bulk of the world's water use is for agriculture, pharma industry, and electricity. So that it is very necessary that we have to use water properly.

Results:-

EXPERIMENT NO. {11}

Object:- To study counseling children on junk foods, balanced diets- using information, education and communication, counseling.

References :-

1) Gupta k. Ashok, "Health Education and community pharmacy", Published by CBS publishers and distributors Pvt. Ltd., Edition~1st 1996.

2) Murgesh N. Health Education and Community Pharmacy, Sataya sai publisher fourth edition reprint in 2006.

Theory:- Results from the physical activity and nutrition in children study ,has given researchers insight into how this type of counseling could be used in the prevention of overweight, type 2 diabetes and cardiovascular diseases in later life. Lifestyle changes, such as improving diet, have been promoted especially during childhood as an effective strategy in the prevention of obesity, type 2 diabetes and cardiovascular diseases.

Contents of Junk Food :-

1) **Additional Sugar**:- various junk food items contain artificially added flavors, colors, and sugars that is not good for the body.

2) **Unhealthy Fats**:- to make their food items that drool worthy, all the food items that fast food restaurants offer, including burgers, hot dogs, sandwiches, and so on ,usually have multiple layers of cheese in them. Most of which is not suitable for children.

3) **Processed substances**

   Harmful effects of junk food on children:-

   1) Reduction in comprehension speed
   2) issues with heart later in life
   3) Growth retardation
   4) Digestion issues
   5) Risk of obesity
   6) Risk of diabetes
   7) Kidney problems
   8) Risk of fatigue
   9) weak circulation
   10) Lower eq

Balanced Diet:- A balanced diet is a diet that contains differing kinds of foods in certain quantities and proportions so that the requirement for calories, proteins, minerals, vitamins and alternative nutrients is adequate and a small provision is reserved for additional nutrients to endure the short length of leanness.

Carbohydrate:- carbohydrate are either simple or complex and are major sources of energy in all human diets . **Examples:-** Glucose, fructose (in fruits), vegetables, glycogen in animal foods.

Proteins:- proteins are primary structural and functional components of every living cells. **Examples:-** Milk , Egg, meat, fish, pulses, legumes etc are rich sources of proteins.

Fats:- Fats are concentrated sources of energy made up of fatty acids in different proportions. **Examples :-** Oils, butter, ghee and other dietary products.

Vitamins:- vitamins are chemical compounds required by the body in a small amounts. **Examples:-** Vit. A, Vit B, Vit. C etc.

Mineral:- inorganic elements found in body fluids and tissues. **Examples:-** sodium, potassium, calcium, phosphorus, copper ,zinc.

Communication Counselling of Children on Junk Food:- Junk food is any highly processed, high in calories and low in nutrients . Junk food is also usually high in added sugars, salts and saturated or trans fats.

Eating a diet high in junk food is linked to a higher risk of obesity, depression, digestive issues, heart diseases, stroke, type 2 diabetes, cancer and early death. So that it is necessary to prevent the use of junk foods in children.

Results :-

EXPERIMENT NO. {12}

Object:-To prepare various chart on nutrients , sources of various nutrients from locally available foods. chart of glycemic index of foods.

References :-

1) Gupta k. Ashok, "Health Education and community pharmacy", Published by CBS publishers and distributors Pvt. Ltd., Edition~1st 1996.

2) Khurana S., Suresh P. and Kaisi R. social pharmacy, s vikas and co.

Theory:-

Glycemic Index:- The GI is a rating system where foods are on a scale of 1 to 100 based on how much they raise blood sugar.

Carbohydrate :- Carbohydrate are either simple or complex and are major sources of energy in all human diets. **Examples :-** Glucose, fructose (in fruits), vegetables, glycogen in animal foods.

Proteins :- proteins are primary structural and functional components of every living cells.

Examples :- Milk , Egg, meat, fish, pulses, legumes etc are rich sources of proteins .

Fats:- Fats are concentrated sources of energy made up of fatty acids in different proportions.

Examples :- Oils, butter, ghee and other dietary products.

Vitamins:- vitamins are chemical compounds required by the body in a small amounts.

Examples:- Vit. A, Vit B, Vit. C etc.

Minerals:- Mineral are inorganic elements found in body fluids and tissues. **Examples:-** sodium, potassium, calcium, phosphorus, copper, zincetc.

Table :- Chart of Glycemic Index of Foods:-

S.NO.	FOODS	GRAMS OF CARBS	GI RANGE	AVERAGE GI
01	White potato	34	56-111	High 80s
02	Sweet potato	24	44-78	61
03	Carrots (1/2 cup)	6	39-54	48
04	Chickpeas (1 cup)	54	31-36	34
05	Apple	15	28-44	40
06	Banana	27	46-70	58
07	White rice	45	39-87	66

Table :- chart on nutrients , sources of various nutrients from locally available foods

Fat soluble vitamins:-

S.NO.	Vitamins and its chemical names	Sources	Deficiency Diseases	Daily Requirments (adults)
01	Vitamin A retinol	Milk, egg, green leafy vegetables.	Stunted growth ,night blindness,xerophthalmia ,keratinization	750 mcg
02	Vitamin D calciferol	Fish liver oils, milk, egg yolk	Rickets ,osteomalacia	2.5 mcg
03	Vitamin E tocopherols	Egg yolk, green vegetabls, nuts,butter	Cystic fibrosis, ataxia,crohn's disease	8-10 mg
04	Vitamin K phylloquinone	Cabbage, fruits,leafy vegetables,	Slow blood clotting ,hemorrhages in new born	70-140 g

Table :- chart on nutrients , sources of various nutrients from locally available foods

water soluble vitamins :-

S.NO.	Vitamins and its chemical names	Sources	Deficiency Diseases	Daily Requirments (adults)
01	Vit. B_1 thiamin	Nuts, legumes yeast, egg yolk	Beri-beri	1-1.5 mg
02	Vit.B_2 Riboflavin	Milk, green vegetables,eggs, liver	Dermatitis ,angular stomatitis	1.5-2 mg
03	Vit. B_6 Pyridoxine	egg yolk ,liver, beans,soyabeans meat	Rarely observed	1-2 mg
04	Folic acid	green vegetables,eggs, liver	Anemia	200 g
05	Nicotinic acid or niacin	Yeast, fish,pulses	Pellegra, Dermatitis, dementia	10-20 mg
06	Pantothenic acid	egg yolk ,liver, green vegetables, liver	Dermatitis, adrenal insufficiency	Unknown
07	Biotin	Yeast, liver, pulses,nuts	Dermatitis,conjuncti vitis	Unknown
08	Vit. C or Ascorbic acid	Citrus fruits, berries,lemon.	Hemorrhages, scurvy,anaemia,slow wound healing.	30-45 mg

Results :-

Object:- To study of tobacco cessation, counseling, identifying various tobacco containing products .

References:-

1) Gupta k. Ashok, "Health Education and community pharmacy", Published by CBS publishers and distributors Pvt. Ltd., Edition~1st 1996.

2) Murgesh N. Health Education and Community Pharmacy, Sataya sai publisher fourth edition reprint in 2006.

Theory:- Tobacco smoke contains nicotine, which is addictive and can cause dependence. As a result, nicotine withdrawal often makes the process of quitting difficult. When tobacco is smoked, nicotine rapidly reaches peak levels in the bloodstream and enters the brain, if the smoke is not directly inhaled into the lungs; nicotine is absorbed through mucous membranes and reaches peak blood levels and the brain more slowly.

Counseling:-

How Do You Control A Tobacco Addiction: - steps to make quitting easier include

1. Pick a stop date
2. Make a list of the reasons why you want to quit…..
3. Keep track of where, when, and why you use tobacco…….
4. Through away all of your tobacco…..
5. Tell your friends that you are quitting….
6. When your stop date arrives date arrives, stop.

   STAGES:- There are 5 stages to quit smoking :-

1. Pre- contemplation (not thinking about quitting)
2. Contemplation (thinking about quitting but not ready to quit)
3. Preparation (getting ready to quit)
4. Action (quitting)
   5. Maintenance (remaining a non- smoker).

<u>Tobacco Containing Products :-</u>

   1. Cigars
   2. Electronic cigarette
   3. Cigarettes

4. Smokeless tobacco

5. Hookah

6. Chewing tobacco

7. Beedi

8. Gutkha

9. Pouch

10. Tobacco pipe

11. Role -your- own cigarette.

<u>Tobacco Related Diseases</u> :-   smoking causes cancer, heart disease, stroke, lung cancer, diabetes, chronic bronchitis , eye diseases.

<u>Harmful Chemicals In Tobacco Products</u> :-

1. Nicotine

2. Hydrogen cyanide

3. Lead

4. Arsenic

5. Benzene etc.

<u>Results :-</u>

EXPERIMENT NO. {14}

Object: To prepare a first aid kit.

References:-

1) Gupta k. Ashok, "Health Education and community pharmacy", Published by CBS publishers and distributors Pvt. Ltd., Edition~1st 1996.

2) Murgesh N. Health Education and Community Pharmacy, Sataya sai publisher fourth edition reprint in 2006.

Theory:

First Aid

First aid is the immediate temporary emergency aid given by a layman to suffer in case of medical emergency. The duty of first aider is to render aid until the arrival of a physician, once the medical practitioner takes the complete charge .The responsibility of the first aider crease. Proper first aid may save the life of patients and reduce his sufferings. Every day may arise anywhere at any time. But as a pharmacist our responsibility is still greater because people expect much more from pharmacist and this is justified in view of the knowledge and training.

The objective of every first aid training program is as follows:-

- ✓ Prevention of accident by mean of safety camping and instructions in the fundamental to first aid whenever possible.
- ✓ Teaching the first aider to determine the appropriate type and extent of injury so that patient suffers minimum harm when the assistance is rendered.
- ✓ Teaching the first aider to act quickly and efficiently in case of an emergency he should know they do and don't of the method of treatment.
- ✓ The essential of first aid are 3Breathing (airway), Bleeding and Brake (fracture)

The most important rules of first aid in order and importance are:-

- Supply oxygen to the lungs
- Stop bleeding
- Prevent and treat shock
- Prevent further injury

Procedure:-

- First is medical attention that is administered a immediately after accident illness occur.
- Take a clean sanitizer box which is available at home.

- Cover it with white sheet
- Draw plus (+) sign with red colour marker on the cap
- Collect the medicine which is primarily available.
- All the material should be clean and fresh.
- Take all the requirements (box, banded, Dettol, antiseptic cream, small scissor, bandage cotton pain killer aspirin, thermometer, sanitizer, oximeter buy it which is not available.
- Average all item in the box properly and systematically.
- Cover box with pullbox.
- Now finally close the box with cap.

Result:

www.ingramcontent.com/pod-product-compliance
Lightning Source LLC
Chambersburg PA
CBHW040157110726
48005CB00018B/2802